THE
DAWNING
John Gilman

"Through the tender mercy of our God,
With which the Dayspring from on high has visited us..."
Luke 1:78, NKJV

Copyright © 2009 Dayspring International
Printed in the United States of America
Published by: Dayspring International
All rights reserved. No part of this book may be reproduced in any form without the written permission of the publishers, except brief quotations used in connection with reviews in magazines or newspapers.

Cover and text art copyright
© 2008 Hampton Creative, Tulsa, OK

Scripture taken from the New King James Version. Copyright © 1982 by Thomas Nelson, Inc. Used by permission. All rights reserved.

Revised and updated previous edition titled
They're Killing an Innocent Man.

Dayspring International

P.O. Box 3309 – Virginia Beach, VA 23454
Telephone: (757) 428-1092
Fax number: (757) 428-0257
Website: www.dayspringinternational.org
Email: info@dayspringinternational.org

DEDICATION

I dedicate this book to my brothers and sisters in India

who have found hope as the dawning of Christ's love has shined on them.

In Him, may they find peace and joy for their hearts . . .

strength for each new day that comes . . .

and undying boldness as they share the light of Christ

among those lost in darkness within their nation.

TABLE OF CONTENTS

ACKNOWLEDGEMENT 5

OCEANS OF MERCY 7

THEY'RE KILLING AN INNOCENT MAN 9

JESUS PUSHED ME 11

LET'S DO IT 15

WHAT ARE THOSE CLOUDS OVER THERE? 17

WHY ARE YOU ONLY JUST NOW COMING TO TELL US? 27

IF YOU CONTINUE ON THIS COURSE 31

YOU MUST BE KIDDING! 33

THE HAPPIEST DAY OF MY LIFE 35

I WAS GOING TO BURN THEIR EQUIPMENT 37

OH, IF I COULD HAVE ONE MORE CRUSADE! 39

A QUANTUM LEAP! 41

TAKE THIS FILM TO EVERY VILLAGE 43

THIS FILM CAN DO MORE 45

ACKNOWLEDGEMENT

Extraordinary events in the kingdom of our Lord Jesus Christ are shared in this book that would not have happened if it were not for some very unusual people. I dedicate *The Dawning* to them.

First, my mother, Marylou, who was bedridden for 15 years, totally deformed by rheumatoid arthritis but still prayed unceasingly for her son to become a minister of the gospel.

Second, my dear wife of 44 years, Caroline, now home with the Lord, whose faith, courage and sacrifice truly helped birth a phenomenal evangelism and church growth movement in India.

And finally, to the hundreds of brave and dedicated Indian men and women who are risking their lives daily, reaping a tremendous harvest of souls in their native land sharing the gospel that has so transformed their own lives.

A typical billboard in India advertises a showing of Dayasagar *(Oceans of Mercy). The film was produced with all native Indian actors.*

ONE

OCEANS OF MERCY

"Stop! Please stop now!"

The taxi driver could speak little English, but he knew what I meant.

What I had just seen on that sultry afternoon in a noisy, palm-leafed village near India's Bay of Bengal brought my life to an abrupt halt. All at once I felt joy, resentment, curiosity, excitement, even betrayal.

Before me was a larger-than-life billboard with a scene I never expected to see — especially in this Hindu-dominated land. There was Jesus, with the crown of thorns piercing His brow, blood flowing down His face, struggling to carry a huge wooden cross. Behind Him were the faces of what seemed like millions of Indian people.

Immediately I realized the billboard was promoting a major motion picture of the life of Christ. In Hindi, the title of the film was *Dayasagar* [pronounced DIE-uh SAW-guh]. I kept asking people, "What does this word mean in English?" "Oceans of Mercy" was the reply.

"O Lord," I cried, "have I come halfway around the world to bring the message of Jesus through motion pictures — only to find it's already been done?"

It was February 1979. I had just resigned from my position as an Executive Producer of the Christian Broadcasting Network. To me, there was no question that I was to produce a film that would reach millions for Christ. But now this!

I looked up and said, "Lord, why didn't You tell me? Am I wasting all my efforts?" I became frightened and confused. It seemed that my whole life was a preparation for making such a film.

On a scrap of paper I wrote the name of the movie house where the film was playing. I rushed back to the home of a missionary friend who spoke the language and said, "We're going to the movies tonight." I had to see it immediately.

The all-Indian cast of our Life of Christ motion picture tells the story of the New Testament, makes it come alive, and has brought many millions to faith in Jesus Christ.

THE DAWNING

TWO

THEY'RE KILLING AN INNOCENT MAN

More than 2,000 people jammed into the cinema house that night. Movies play an important role in India. I had spent numerous hours and countless days watching Indian films, analyzing their production, trying to find a strategy for the dream the Lord had planted and nurtured in my heart.

Tonight, however, was completely different. I wasn't thinking about lights, cameras or action. I was pondering two things: Why was I here? What was God trying to tell me?

Was I going to see a perversion of the gospel? Could an Indian film company really tell the story of Jesus? Had some missionary organization "stolen" the dream God had given me? All sorts of questions entered my mind as I walked into the theatre.

We made our way to the balcony, where the best seats are always found. The lights in the theatre dimmed, and the projector flooded the screen with the production. From the beginning, I kept asking my friend, "Is it biblical? Are they telling the real story?"

"Oh, it is good. It's really good," he kept assuring me.

Within the first 10 minutes I realized that someone had done his homework. The all-Indian cast was telling the story of the New Testament and making it come alive to people of another culture.

The audience was totally absorbed. Jesus, it seemed, was more than an actor on the screen. The people loved Him and identified with the Savior, and were desperate for His heart and compassion.

The crowd in the theatre that night was both noisy and interactive. They cheered when Jesus drove the money-changers out of the temple. When He healed the blind man and the leper, they broke into applause. Other times they would laugh with joy or sigh with relief or even cry softly as they sat in their chairs. But, in the next moments of the film, I was taken by surprise, not fully prepared for what was coming.

My heart was overwhelmed as I saw what happened in the hearts of the people when Jesus was crucified on the cross. People all across the movie house began to shout, "They're killing an innocent man!" Many actually screamed for the soldiers to stop. As the nails were driven into Jesus' hands and feet, their emotions changed from anger to sadness. Many wept openly, shocked and despondent at what was happening to the Son of God. The soft glow from the screen allowed me to see scores of tear-stained faces.

· This was not like a gospel-hardened American audience that knew what would happen next. They had not experienced a lifetime bombardment of daily Christian radio and television. Many had never even heard of Jesus and were caught by surprise at the unfolding events.

When Christ rose from the dead, the audience whistled and clapped their hands for joy. They were wild with happiness when they saw that Jesus was alive.

As for my response? I couldn't control my tears as I saw the effect of the gospel in this faraway land. My mind was racing with all kinds of thoughts.

When the nearly three-hour production ended with Christ's ascension, all I could do was sit there paralyzed — almost dumbfounded — while the people filed out. I was drained emotionally from all that I had experienced in such a short time. Finally I turned to my friend and said, "This is the most powerful tool of evangelism I have ever seen." He agreed.

Again I was confronted with the troubling thought: What am I going to do? The film has already been made!

My ego almost prevented me from understanding the extraordinary miracle of what I had just witnessed.

Then God said to me, "John, I have not only sent you to India, but I have prepared the way."

THREE

JESUS PUSHED ME

As the great film came to a close, I looked closely at the credits. The role of Jesus was portrayed by the same man who produced it — Vijay Chandar.

"How can I find the producer of *Dayasagar*?" I asked my Indian friend. "It's urgent that I meet him immediately."

After a week of searching, we were finally given a phone number for Vijay Chandar's production company. He lived in Madras, a major city in the state of Tamil Nadu, on India's southeast coast.

When he came to the phone I said, "This is John Gilman from the United States. I have seen your movie, and I like it very much. May I talk with you about it? Can we meet somewhere? It's very important to me."

I was encouraged by the enthusiasm in his voice as he responded, "Let's meet at the Madras Airport." I purchased a ticket and rushed to meet him.

I couldn't wait to learn how he had managed to produce such an authentic account of the life of Christ. How had he achieved such a remarkable distribution of this film in the Hindu theatre system?

Vijay was not hard to pick out of the crowd. He was about 6-feet-2-inches tall and smartly dressed in a Nehru-style white suit. His black hair was down to his shoulders, much like when he played the role of Jesus. His eyes were brown and steely. I had seen him on the screen, but he was much more impressive in person.

Later, I learned that Vijay was one of India's top producers and actors, best known for playing "tough guy roles."

His chauffeur drove us to the restaurant of a local hotel. I was anxious to know everything possible about this Hindu filmmaker. The moment we were seated at the table I began to bombard him with questions about Oceans of Mercy.

As we talked, I found out that for more than five years he

had worked on the film. The group that started the project soon ran out of money, and the production faced total cancellation. Vijay, determined to complete the movie, found new financing, picked up the pieces and continued.

"Vijay, why did you make that film?" I asked. His answer surprised me.

"Jesus pushed me to do it," was his reply. "Something would not let the project die. I could not escape from it. The hand of God was steering my every move."

A Hindu all of his life, he was of the Brahman caste, the highest rung of their spiritual ladder. "I believed that Jesus was a good teacher but nothing more. When the opportunity to make a movie on the life of Christ came to me, I was drawn to it by an inner compulsion I did not understand," he said.

"The project had many problems, but I could not stop the production," Vijay told me. "It was as if God were making the film, and I had no choice."

I looked directly into his eyes and said, "I have no choice either in what I am about to say. Jesus is compelling me to tell you to give me this motion picture. I want to take it to every village in India."

It was only then, at that very moment, that I knew exactly why I left a great ministry, sold my home, risked my entire future and came halfway around the world. I didn't care about the rights; the bottom line was that I wanted the film for evangelism. My heart skipped a beat as I sat there before Vijay and thought, "Please don't prohibit me from taking this movie everywhere, because one way or another, by the grace of God, I'm going to do it."

I told him, "As surely as God has chosen you to produce this major motion picture of the life of Christ, God has chosen me to see that this film is presented in every village and hamlet in India — even if it is out in an open field with a portable projector."

To my amazement, Vijay agreed: "John, I believe that your Christ has sent you here for just that purpose." He did not realize at that moment how important that truth would become in his life.

Vijay was having great success getting his film shown in movie houses, and by India's standards, it was a strong box-office attraction, but he did not have the vision for saturating the nation. That was to become my role.

Only about 20 percent of India's population live in the big cities; the remaining 80 percent live in over 600,000 villages where there are few theatres. By traditional methods, these villagers would never have the chance to encounter what millions were experiencing in the darkened theatres of the cities.

By the time we first met, over five million people had already heard the gospel through this dramatic film, which was produced with an all-Indian cast and initially released in the Telugu language. For biblical accuracy, Vijay had sought the advice of a Christian theologian. The production breaks down all cultural barriers. Jesus is not presented as the "white man's God." He is Indian. If He were to walk out of Nazareth into a typical village in India, He would be one of them — looking as they look, wearing similar clothing, drawing water from a well, walking the dusty roads as they do today. Almost everything would be the same. The one "who had no place to lay His head" would be loved by India's masses. If any film was on target for true, life-changing evangelism, this was certainly it.

In India, common conveyances may share uncommonly good news! In this case, a rickshaw advertises Dayasagar, *our Life of Christ film showing.*

THE DAWNING

FOUR

LET'S DO IT

"We've got it! We've got it!" I shouted to my dear Indian friend Ernest, a great Christian leader. "We have worked out the film rights agreement!"

Without any delay, we began intensive planning sessions on how to reach the 600,000 villages of India with the gospel through this amazing film. Our strategy was to use mobile film teams in rural areas and at the same time intensify our efforts to continue showing it in the cities. Each team would consist of four people, a van, a movie projector, a screen, a portable generator, a loudspeaker and a copy of the film.

We envisioned that the van would drive through the village the day of the showing and announce that the film would be presented at an outdoor location that night. There would be a public invitation for people to accept Christ, and if there was no church in the village, one would be established for the new believers.

"Hallelujah!" I said. "Let's do it!" We named the project Dayspring International.

I could see the light dawning on India. What was that light? Certainly it was the Son of God, the Dayspring — the promise of the noonday sun soon to appear. But, I could also visualize the powerful light of a projector on a screen shining into the darkened hearts of villagers everywhere. God had shown me this very movie in a vision a decade earlier, and now we were about to show it in a village for the first time.

Thankfully, I was able to purchase a 16mm projector with the help of ministry friends that believed in this mission. The Lord was bringing everything together. How exciting!

It was in Amalapuram, in the state of Andhra Pradesh — a hot, humid area thick with coconut palms, mango trees and lush flowers, where our first showing took place. A painted movie poster hung on the back of a rickshaw as the driver pedaled through the village announcing the movie over a loud speaker.

I asked my local hosts to take me to a tailor. They drove to a market where I could find the best in town.

"Sir, I want you to sew me a big movie screen out of bed sheets. I want it 20 feet wide and 20 feet high. And I need it quick."

Within minutes, the little man was almost buried in white cloth at his foot-powered sewing machine. What a beautiful screen he made! It was exactly what we needed.

With our new screen in hand, we went to the site of our first showing. We dug holes in the ground, put in two large bamboo poles and strung up the sewn-together sheets. People were already gathering as I tested the new projector, the film and the sound system.

FIVE

WHAT ARE THOSE CLOUDS OVER THERE?

Huge, black swirling clouds caught my eye as I was making some final preparations for the film. They were headed directly our way. It looked like a monsoon. "What are those clouds over there?" I gasped. Within minutes the palm trees were bending, and I thought the sheets would rip from the bamboo poles.

"Lord," I prayed, "I've come all this way, the people are arriving, and now we're going to be washed out. Please, Lord, stop the rain!" But the storm continued to build.

I was fretting, as it was just 10 minutes before the film showing was about to start. I also decided to give the projector one last check to make sure it was lined up perfectly on the screen. When I turned it on, another worker simultaneously plugged in the amplifier, and the projection bulb blew on the projector.

"I don't have a spare bulb! It looks as if we're finished before we even begin," I told a helper nearby.

Dejected, discouraged and distraught, I walked down the path where some of my Indian friends were sitting and said, "God's got to do a miracle. He's got to heal a light bulb and shield us with a big umbrella, or we won't be showing this film."

One of the problems wasn't so monumental after all. I found the projector manual, opened the booklet and read, "If the bulb fails, turn the circuit breaker on after waiting two minutes."

"Lord, let this be it," I said as I finally flipped the switch. I shouted for joy when light flooded the screen.

Now we just needed a monsoon-sized miracle to divert the storm. The crowd was building fast. First 500. Then 1,000. The huge screen itself was a big attraction for the village.

At 8:00 p.m. I turned to my friend and said, "How many people are here?"

"It looks like about twenty-five hundred," he said, smiling broadly.

But then, big, hot drops of rain began falling from the dense, blackened sky. I looked up and said, "In the name of Jesus, I command these clouds to leave. I want three hours of clear weather."

God answered my prayer . . . the raindrops stopped the moment the projector began.

For the next three hours, I did not watch the story on the makeshift screen. Instead, I studied the emotions of the people . . . the tears of sorrow, the sighs, the smiles of joy, and the agonizing cries as Christ was crucified. Would their reaction be the same as those in the theatre? Would they laugh and cry and be deeply moved by the story?

Yes, the huge crowd identified with Jesus from beginning to end. I stood there in the darkness, praising God for what was happening.

At the conclusion of the film, a national minister invited the people of Amalapuram to make a commitment to the Lord Jesus Christ. Hundreds responded — people of every age and occupation, children, mothers, fathers, businessmen, even criminals and prostitutes. In my heart, I was confident that this scene would be repeated thousands of times.

Five minutes after the service ended, a torrential rain flooded the meeting site.

But God even used the rain for His glory. The next day, at a nearby river, the local pastors held a giant water baptismal service for some 200 new believers.

Dayspring's Founder John Gilman prays with one of our first mobile film teams as they prepare to show Dayasagar.

When viewers see Jesus in Dayasagar, *our all-Indian acted Life of Christ motion picture, they receive faith that He can bring hope to them, too!*

An Indian man touched by our Life of Christ film receives prayer from one of our film team leaders.

A new believer rejoices over her new-found faith in Christ because of the witness of our Life of Christ motion picture.

Our all-Indian acted Life of Christ motion picture presents a vivid portrayal of every aspect of Christ's life and death ... and has touched the lives of millions of Indian people!

THE DAWNING

John Gilman presents our mobile film team workers with the smaller, lighter DVD equipment. The old 16-mm film equipment was bulky and cumbersome.

God's Word is a strength and shield for the believers of India.

Another new believer declares through water baptism her commitment to Christ.

Our pastors have launched more than 2,500 Good Shepherd Community Churches across India, helping to disciple thousands.

THE DAWNING

When watching Dayasagar, *many weep openly at what is happening to the Son of God.*

Millions have come to Christ and are being baptized into the faith. New believers may travel long distances to be baptized — as many as 700 have undergone baptism in one day!

THE DAWNING

Like Shandar, the thief in the story you'll read about on page 29, here is another joyful believer whose life and circumstances were transformed by the gospel.

SIX

WHY ARE YOU ONLY JUST NOW COMING TO TELL US?

Back in America in 1981, I could hardly believe the reports from India whenever I opened the mail. Even without abundant finances, Indian pastors found ways to take scratchy prints of the film and managed to show it in the villages. Week after week, the letters kept coming. Salvation reports were soon coming in by the thousands. The letters we received from the mobile film team leaders told amazing stories, just like this one from East India: "On the outskirts of Vijayawada is a slum called Payakapurnam. People who went to the film for the first time wanted to see it again and again to build up their faith in Jesus. Now a new church has been established, and John Babu is the pastor."

In a communist-controlled village, the chief of the village allowed the film to be shown to almost 3,500 people. Nearly 400 gave their hearts to Christ, and a church was built. Some villagers asked our film teams, "Jesus lived so long ago — why are you only just now coming to tell us this good news?"

In Ulunderpet, the film was so requested that it was shown seven times! It was followed by a short crusade, and a church was born with 75 people attending on the very first day. Without the film, it would normally have taken a missionary at least two or three years to establish a church of this size in the area.

Each new church that arises from a film showing is made up of individual souls whom Jesus has touched in a personal way. Let me share a few of their stories.

The leper's story

Ven Katuratam was a leper covered from head to toe with oozing sores. He had been a fisherman until the dreaded disease struck his body. He was confined to a hut, separated from his dear wife and children, and fed like an animal under the door. One night, he managed to sneak out after hearing a loud speaker announcement for the film showing. He had never seen a film before. Slipping along the shadows of the buildings and huts, he hid in the darkness watching the story of Jesus. When he saw Jesus heal the leper as he watched the film, he couldn't believe his eyes. After the film showing he sought the pastor.

"Can this Jesus help me?" he pleaded desperately. The pastor led Ven Katuratam to Christ that evening. Through prayer and treatment over a period of time, the leprosy healed. Even though many physical scars remain, there is such joy in his face because he is happily working again, reunited with his family, and, most of all, he wants to be a witness for Jesus to other lepers.

The farmer's story

A farmer named Shamar told how a flood came and destroyed everything he had. "With my head aching and spinning," he said, "I walked toward the river. By the time I reached the water, I had made up my mind to kill myself by jumping into the river and drowning. At least my wife could then take the children and go to live with her father. Somehow it didn't matter to me that by Hindu custom I would be doomed to return to earth as an insect or some despised animal. That evening everyone seemed to be heading toward a flat, grassy area on the other side of the river, so I followed to see what was happening. It was a film being shown, and I said to myself, 'The river can wait.'

I had never heard about Jesus before this film. I could hardly believe my eyes. He performed miracles and even raised the dead. This Jesus was not put off by the darkest problem or the worst situation. Instead He turned the darkness into light. That's what He did for me that night, and since then, for my wife too. A new church has started in my village, and we all encourage each other. Thank God for that film and for giving my family a new life."

The priest's story

Veda was his village temple's "holy man." Every morning, Veda would open the temple with the loud clanging of bells and the burning of incense. People brought sacrifices to the gods, praying for rain or good crops. He said, "One day a van pulled into the field next to my temple. The man asked if he could plug his electrical cord into my outlet. It seemed harmless enough, so I let him. The film they showed in the street that night was about Jesus Christ and how He provided the supreme sacrifice — that no other sacrifice would be needed to make me clean. During the scenes of the crucifixion, I began to cry and couldn't stop."

The thief's story

Shandar and George were thieves just out of prison. One night they saw a crowd of people gathering, and they decided this would be a good opportunity for them to steal.

"It was something we could not pass up," Shandar said. "We were sure most of the village people would be there, and we decided that their homes would be empty, so we could go and rob them. We stood in the back. As soon as the film started, we saw that this was no ordinary film. It was about a man named Jesus. He was able to change people. I had the strangest feeling. Both George and I stayed after the film and asked Jesus to change us. We wanted to be like Him."

Shandar and George started looking for work the next day. They are involved with the newly established church in their village, and it is evident to all that if Jesus Christ can change hardened criminals like them, He can change anyone.

Jeyapaul's transformation is amazing: he began his professional life as a contract killer ... today he is a dedicated film equipment manager.

SEVEN

IF YOU CONTINUE ON THIS COURSE

I returned to India to find people everywhere ready to join the teams. The first showing we had in the slums of Bombay attracted some 3,000 people — plus plenty of pigs and chickens. Our screen was a bed sheet stretched between the second floors of two shacks near a little square. An open sewer ran through the area, and the ground was wet and spongy. Even in the midst of that filth, hundreds came forward for salvation.

My enthusiasm for the vision became contagious. God sent funds from many unexpected sources. God's hand was at work! The ministry friends grew from 30 to 300 and then to 3,000! Pat Robertson shared with his 700 Club television audience what was happening, and people across America began to undergird the project. He said, "John, if you continue on this course, all of that great nation will be evangelized indeed!"

We couldn't contain the enthusiasm in our hearts. Finally, we had found a medium to reach the mass audiences with the gospel of Jesus Christ! Film is perhaps the most persuasive tool of communication on earth. And, in India, people are crazy about films. Other methods of evangelism have their place, but none is more effective in such a short period of time.

In the months that followed, we saw thousands of souls come to Christ and churches spring up week after week as a result of our follow-up programs. And, before long, many of the new Christians became propagators of the gospel themselves. Jeyapaul is one of our most dynamic young leaders, who oversees the purchase, maintenance, and distribution of our video systems to all of the teams. The night he saw *Dayasagar*, he had been hired as a contract killer and was on his way to kill a man.

"I already had 50,000 rupees with me as a down payment," says Jeyapaul. But Jesus took his heart captive! He returned the money and joined a film team.

When Founder John Gilman travels to village film showings with the teams, he usually stays in the vehicle so as not to attract attention — in many remote villages, a white man would be an oddity.

EIGHT
YOU MUST BE KIDDING!

Our film, *Dayasagar*, which was shot on location in India with an all-Indian cast, usually gives our team an open door. When the audience looks up at the screen and sees Jesus heal the leper, they say, "This must be true. These are our people telling the story." Many times, after a film showing, they ask, "What village does Jesus come from?"

Not only do we provide a film in their language, produced in their country — but we also insist that every member of our film team be an Indian pastor, evangelist or lay person — not a foreigner.

Someone once told me, "John, it must be exciting to stand up after the film and give an invitation or greet the people."

"You must be kidding!" I said.

When I go to the location of a *Dayasagar* showing, I stay in the van — sometimes slumped down in the front seat — until it is completely dark so the people won't see me and be distracted. Only then do I get out for a little while and stand quietly in the shadows to see the people respond to the film. After every film showing, we have one of our team members give an invitation to accept Christ in that village's language. Here is an example of one of our team members' invitation to the vast film audience: "Friends, our holy books tell us that without the shedding of blood there is no forgiveness of sins. But it is not the shedding of the blood of pigs, chickens and goats which can save us, but the blood of Someone very special. And that Someone you have seen tonight. He is God's Son, who shed His own blood for your sin. Will you receive God's sacrifice for you and not shed the blood of animals again?"

When the film is nearly over, I get back in the vehicle until the crowd has departed. Why should a foreigner become a barrier to people about to accept Christ? Not only that, but my presence could arouse anti-Western mobs who might attack the film teams and persecute people who accepted Christ.

A film team leader counts it a joy that he was found worthy to suffer persecution for the cause of Christ. Our teams are often threatened, even attacked, by radicals opposed to the gospel.

NINE

THE HAPPIEST DAY OF MY LIFE

A gang of militants tried to stop Sam's team from showing the film by beating him with bamboo poles and chasing him into his van. They smashed his windows and shoved him through the broken glass until Sam was bloodied and crumpled on the front seat. Then the gang pushed the van toward a deep ravine. But Sam was able to turn the ignition key, and the engine started. He sped away and escaped with his life.

Sam said, "That was the happiest day of my life. I was counted worthy to take a beating for Jesus." He continued, "I didn't want to tell my family about it. My father is a pastor, and I was afraid he would tell me to leave this dangerous work and come back home. When I finally did write to him, he wrote a letter back to me saying, 'I have been a pastor for 40 years, and in all that time I have never had the privilege of being beaten for the gospel.'"

The reason the militant Hindus are increasing the attacks and persecution is that the villagers so readily receive our teams. We discovered a way, with a real Indian film, to tear down all of the cultural barriers that missionaries had to stare in the face through the years. At last, the villagers can now see that Jesus is not just the foreigners' god.

Mark came as an enemy to chase the film team away — but discovered in the film a Savior who would dramatically transform his life. Today, Mark is one of our Good Shepherd Community Church pastors.

THE DAWNING

TEN

I WAS GOING TO BURN THEIR EQUIPMENT

The team concept is the heart of all we do. New team members are immersed in discipleship training and Biblical study for four years. During this time, they show the film three to seven times a week. They learn to pray for the sick, and they develop leadership skills. Their experience makes them ready to step in as pastors, teachers, evangelists and leaders especially in new churches.

One young man named Mark was assigned by his father to perform the daily idol worship in his upper-caste home. He was angry to hear of Christians coming to his village, and he went out to chase them away.

"I was going to burn their equipment," he said. But the film captivated him, and he believed in the Jesus he saw on the screen. His father kicked him out of the village. He was determined to join our film team and went through rigorous on-the-job ministry training for five years.

He is now a powerful pastor in a Good Shepherd Community Church. Day and night he was mentored and trained in fellowship with other team members. They studied and prayed together. They shared one another's burdens. They held each other accountable, and essentially, they became his new family.

I asked him, "How long did you study to become a pastor?"
"Five years," he said.
"And how many times do you think you showed film on the life of Christ?"
"Uncountable," he said, rolling his eyes and laughing.
"I can say 'uncountable!'"

Day by day, Mark absorbed the words and the person of Jesus as he was showing the film and being trained. Today he is a spiritual leader of several hundred people. It just doesn't get any better than this. We are not just blitzing across India with the film. We are building Christian leaders for tomorrow.

Someone had the vision to sponsor the team that reached this young man — at a cost of only $6,000 per year — including their living expenses and their studies. Now he is a mentor to other young men and women. Dayspring's plan is Jesus' method. His team was a few selected men. He imparted his life into them. They went out and multiplied and became self-perpetuating!

ELEVEN

OH, IF I COULD HAVE JUST ONE MORE CRUSADE!

As soon as it became clear that this film, in less than three hours, could impart both an awareness of Christianity and an understanding of the fundamentals of the gospel to so many people, I wanted to duplicate a thousand films and buy a thousand vans.

Our only obstacle, however, was the money we so desperately needed to keep pressing on in the calling that God had set before us.

At that time, the film needed to be translated into all 14 of the major languages of India. Besides needing support for more film teams, more copies of the film, and more vehicles, Dayspring also had to pay the remaining balance involved with obtaining the legal rights to the film. We could move forward immediately if we had $85,000, but that was an enormous mountain for us to climb.

I gathered the family around me in our home in Virginia Beach and asked them to pray. "I've got to have $85,000 in 30 days," I told my wife and two young sons, "or we will lose the opportunity to get these film rights. I'm going to be visiting people to ask for their help, and I'm not coming back until I get it."

On that journey I went to the first person, the second and then the third, and so on. The answer was always the same, "We can't help you." It was so easy to become discouraged. Yet, at the same time, I was more determined than ever.

Then the twelfth person brought hope to my heart when he said, "I'm on the board of Mark Buntain's ministry. I believe he can do something for you. Right now he's in Missouri, where he's been very ill. I'll call him and tell him about you."

"You can also tell him I'm on my way to see him," I replied.

Mark Buntain's Mission of Mercy to Calcutta built scores of churches, fed hundreds of thousands of starving children, and built numerous hospitals and orphanages.

He was alone in his apartment. His fingers were curled

and twitching with immense pain from a spinal operation. His excruciating pain was evident as I sat and talked with him. But as I told him about our film, he stood to his feet and paced the small room back and forth.

He started weeping and praising God. Then he said, "John, if I had $85,000, I'd give it to you right now. But I do have $35,000 that the board of my ministry wants me to use for crusades in India." He said, "Oh, if I could have just one more crusade! But I'm just too ill to go. Can you come out to Tacoma, Washington, to the next meeting of our board? I'm going to ask them to give you the $35,000 for the Hindi film."

"I'll be there, Dr. Buntain."

At that important meeting, his board asked dozens of questions about our vision to reach India with the gospel. Then they said, "Let us pray about this tonight. We'll let you know our decision tomorrow."

The next day one of the board members gave me the answer I was longing for. He exclaimed, "We want to help. We are going to give you $35,000 now and loan you $50,000 so you can start the work immediately."

When I came home, bouncing through the door after being gone only 15 days, my little son said, "We prayed pretty good, didn't we, Daddy?"

Thank God for Mark Buntain. Mark Buntain is in heaven now. But because of his investment in the people of India, he will soon be surrounded by millions of Hindi-speaking souls. Yes, there was "one more crusade" — his biggest one. And even today, the legacy continues.

TWELVE

A QUANTUM LEAP!

How could I know that a dusty ride over some winding, bumpy village roads would impact the spread of the gospel dramatically? I had been to a conference with scores of Christian leaders from across India, and I was wishing I could personally meet Dr. Joseph D'souza, the famous Indian leader who headed up Operation Mobilization India. And there we were, just as God ordained it, packed in next to each other, inside a steamy 15-passenger van.

During the five-hour trip to the airport, I poured out my heart to Dr. D'souza. I knew that he wanted, as I did, to reach all of India in the most effective and efficient way possible. Both of us were using mobile teams. Operation Mobilization specialized in recruiting and sending young Indian men and women into the cities and villages to spread the good news of Jesus Christ through the written word.

He knew of the success of our film within the villages. He was struggling with the desire to reach as many as possible but knew that so many could not read. We were also concerned about duplicating efforts.

As we neared our destination, Dr. D'souza turned to me and said, "Let's join together!"

That was the climactic moment — truly a quantum leap — for both our ministries. Today the partnership has more than 1400 national workers, supports some 226 teams and is still growing each year.

One of our film teams travels to bring our Life of Christ film to another village!

THE DAWNING

THIRTEEN

TAKE THIS FILM INTO EVERY VILLAGE

"Take this film into every village of India." Such a simple piece of direction . . . such a life-transforming calling. This was what the Holy Spirit gave me that first day when I met with Vijay Chandar. At the time, I did not fully understand the powerful wisdom hidden in those few words. And, taking the film into the villages led to another amazing and unexpected development.

Because we formed film teams and sent them out with mobile equipment, village by village, to our surprise a wonderful method of church planting was born. So many people have come to faith in Christ that our leaders have had to organize church planting teams as well as film teams.

The film teams are the heart of all we do in India. Every step of Jesus' master plan to build His church is incorporated in the team concept. It is how people are won to Christ. It is where we recruit and train leaders. It is the catalyst for planting new churches.

As of 2008, in our Good Shepherd Community Church group, we have over 2500 churches of 30 or more people each — and more are added every month.

When I stop and reflect on all that God has done within the past 29 years of ministry, I can't help but be astounded. The objective is to have the villagers look upon the screen and digest more gospel in two and a half hours than anyone could get in a year of preaching or teaching. Visualizing the gospel is such a powerful communication tool . . . and thankfully, with the Lord's help, this tool has propelled Dayspring to where it is today.

The teachings of Jesus Christ are brand new to many Indian people, and services in our Good Shepherd Community Churches are often packed with new believers eager to grow in Christ.

FOURTEEN

THIS FILM CAN DO MORE

In the fall of 2007, I was invited to a conference sponsored by the International Orality Network.

"Orality?" I wondered. "What's that?" I knew that 70 percent of the six billion people in the world cannot read, do not read or will not read. They are oral communicators and oral learners. Most of the villagers who see this film belong in this majority. For them, this movie is more powerful than any written word because it communicates visually and orally. It tells them a memorable story that can be retold orally again and again.

But in this conference, leaders of major respected ministries were embracing the reality of oral communication in a new way. They were saying with new found confidence that the Bible is actually 75 percent stories, which appeal to oral learners, and that Jesus told stories. They were reaffirming the Master's way of communicating. Matthew 13:34 says that Jesus did not say anything without using a story.

Avery Willis, a prominent Southern Baptist mission leader, said with tears, "We've been doing it all wrong. We have come at the world from our literate, logical, Western-thinking view. We've tried to get those two-thirds of the world to line up with us. We have failed to fulfill the Great Commission because we have not done it the way Jesus taught us to do it. He was a storyteller."

That was the very same conviction I had since the founding of Dayspring International. It was in a prayer time in 1973 that I first heard the Holy Spirit say to me, "I want you to do what I did when I was on earth. I spoke to the people in parables and stories. You do the same." This is clearly God's idea of communication.

In the early years of our ministry, Vijayan Pavamani, a member of the Lausanne Committee for World Evangelization, told me, "We have been praying for a way to reach the masses of India. This film makes it possible."

It is also one of the most cost effective and efficient

investments of dollars in missions today. One day I sat with a calculator and figured what it cost to reach one person. I was astounded — just about 10 cents per soul. What could be a better investment?

Before he passed, Dr. Mark Buntain declared, "This film can do more to reach India's millions for Christ than all other past efforts combined."

That's a bold statement from a man who gave 30 years of his life in Calcutta.

I am extremely humbled and truly amazed at all that God has done so far through Dayspring within the past 29 years of ministry. What an honor and privilege to be a part of winning souls to the Lord's Kingdom ... to be fulfilling the command of the Great Commission! In July of 2007, we celebrated a great milestone of over 10 million souls coming to Christ. Our teams have wholeheartedly worked countless days and hours through all sorts of conditions to reach 246,260 villages so far. Our all-Indian acted Life of Christ motion picture has been seen by over 136,824,000 people. On a monthly average, 2,260 villages are touched with the message of the gospel, and each year, 27,120 annual film showings are changing the hearts of men and women all across the nation. The Spirit of God is springing forth through the nation of India.

Tonight, thousands of Indians will gather to watch *Dayasagar* — from Tamil Nadu in the south to Uttar Pradesh in the north. But there are still 353,740 villages that are waiting for the film to come. There are still hundreds of millions of people waiting to be reached with the gospel of Jesus Christ. Our mission and responsibility, here at Dayspring International, is to take this film into every village in India. With the help of wonderful people like you, we will see millions of new people this year experience the gospel of Jesus Christ through this life-changing film.

If you would like more information, please contact:
Dayspring International
P.O. Box 3309
Virginia Beach, VA 23454
Telephone: (757) 428-1092
Fax Number: (757) 428-0257
Email: info@dayspringinternational.org
Website: www.dayspringinternational.org